ANIMAL SAFARI

Orangutans

by Megan Borgert-Spaniol

BELLWETHER MEDIA • MINNEAPOLIS, MN

Note to Librarians, Teachers, and Parents:

Blastoff! Readers are carefully developed by literacy experts and combine standards-based content with developmentally appropriate text.

Level 1 provides the most support through repetition of high-frequency words, light text, predictable sentence patterns, and strong visual support.

Level 2 offers early readers a bit more challenge through varied simple sentences, increased text load, and less repetition of high-frequency words.

Level 3 advances early-fluent readers toward fluency through increased text and concept load, less reliance on visuals, longer sentences, and more literary language.

Level 4 builds reading stamina by providing more text per page, increased use of punctuation, greater variation in sentence patterns, and increasingly challenging vocabulary.

Level 5 encourages children to move from "learning to read" to "reading to learn" by providing even more text, varied writing styles, and less familiar topics.

Whichever book is right for your reader, Blastoff! Readers are the perfect books to build confidence and encourage a love of reading that will last a lifetime!

This edition first published in 2014 by Bellwether Media, Inc.

No part of this publication may be reproduced in whole or in part without written permission of the publisher. For information regarding permission, write to Bellwether Media, Inc., Attention: Permissions Department, 5357 Penn Avenue South, Minneapolis, MN 55419.

Library of Congress Cataloging-in-Publication Data

Borgert-Spaniol, Megan, 1989-
  Orangutans / by Megan Borgert-Spaniol.
    p. cm. – (Blastoff! readers. Animal safari)
  Summary: "Developed by literacy experts for students in kindergarten through grade three, this book introduces orangutans to young readers through leveled text and related photos"– Provided by publisher.
  Audience: K to grade 3.
  Includes bibliographical references and index.
  ISBN 978-1-60014-913-9 (hardcover : alk. paper)
  1. Orangutan–Juvenile literature. I. Title. II. Series: Blastoff! readers. 1, Animal safari.
  QL737.P96B635 2014
  599.88'3–dc23
                                                                                    2013000880

Contents

What Are Orangutans?

Orangutans are **great apes**. They have long arms and reddish hair.

Tree Life

Orangutans live in **rain forests**. They are the largest **mammals** that live in trees.

They use their
strong arms
to swing from
branches.
They grab them
with their hands
and feet.

Orangutans sleep in trees. They build nests out of branches.

Sometimes they travel on the ground. They move around on their hands and feet.

Food

Orangutans **forage** for food during the day. They eat fruits, leaves, and **shoots**.

Sometimes they eat **insects**. They use sticks to pick **termites** out of termite mounds.

Mother and Baby

A young orangutan lives with its mother for up to eight years.

The mother carries her baby from tree to tree. Hold tight!

21

Glossary

forage—to go out in search of food

great apes—smart mammals that can walk on two feet and grab with their hands; orangutans, gorillas, and chimpanzees are great apes.

insects—small animals with six legs and hard outer bodies; insect bodies are divided into three parts.

mammals—warm-blooded animals that have backbones and feed their young milk

rain forests—warm, wet forests that get a lot of rain

shoots—plants that are just beginning to grow

termites—insects that feed on wood

To Learn More

AT THE LIBRARY

Ganeri, Anita. *Orangutan*. Chicago, Ill.: Heinemann Library, 2011.

Hughes, Monica. *Orangutan Baby*. New York, N.Y.: Bearport Pub. Co., 2006.

Taylor, Barbara. *Apes and Monkeys*. New York, N.Y.: Kingfisher, 2004.

ON THE WEB

Learning more about orangutans is as easy as 1, 2, 3.

1. Go to www.factsurfer.com.

2. Enter "orangutans" into the search box.

3. Click the "Surf" button and you will see a list of related Web sites.

With factsurfer.com, finding more information is just a click away.

Index

The images in this book are reproduced through the courtesy of: Sergey Uryadnikov, front cover; Fiona Rogers/ Nature Picture Library, p. 5; Tuomas Lehtinen, p. 7; Theo Allof/ Glow Images, p. 9; Cryil Ruoso/ Minden Pictures, p. 11; Huetter, C/ Age Fotostock, p. 13; Christian Hutter/ imag/ imagebroker.net/ SuperStock, p.15; Jaroslaw Grudzinski, p. 15 (left); Irin-k, p. 15 (middle); Subbotina Anna, p. 15 (right); NHPA/ SuperStock, p. 17; Minden Pictures/ SuperStock, p. 19; David Pike/ Nature Picture Library, p. 21.